Modest!

978-0-00-748756-1
1 3 5 7 9 10 8 6 4 2
First published in the UK by HarperCollins Children's Books in 2012

Text by Sarah Delmege
Design by Emily Smyth
Production by Sian Smith
Photography by Dean Freeman

Printed and Bound in Italy

LITTLE MIX

THE OFFICIAL ANNUAL 2013

HarperCollins *Children's Books*

LITTLE MIX

CONTENTS

LITTLE MIX

THE ONLY WAY you won't have heard of Little Mix is if you've been living on a secluded desert island with no internet, radio, TV, newspapers or magazines for the past year. The four girls with the very big voices have taken the whole country by storm. Little Mix fever is everywhere and it's only going to get crazier.

Perrie Edwards, Leigh-Anne Pinnock, Jesy Nelson and Jade Thirlwall are the kind of girls that could be in your class at school, the ones that everyone wants to be friends with. They're exactly what they seem – completely genuine,

incredibly down-to-earth individuals who also happen to be extraordinarily talented. Little Mix might look like any other normal girls, but they're living proof that if you're prepared to work hard, dreams really can come true.

While their fame seems to have come astoundingly quickly, they've put an incredible amount of effort into their success. Even before they became Little Mix the popstars, they'd spent plenty of time working towards their ambition. They've worked hard to make it. So let's celebrate the official Little Mix story...

THE PERFECT MIX
PERRIE

PERRIE EDWARDS

HOMETOWN: South Shields.

STAR SIGN: Cancer.

SHOPAHOLIC: Perrie's favourite stores are Topshop and Urban Outfitters.

SECRET TALENT: She does a pretty good impression of a goat.

BEFORE THE X FACTOR: Perrie was a student and was planning to begin a performing arts degree.

FIRST AUDITION: *You Oughta Know* by Alanis Morissette.

MOST EMBARRASSING MOMENT: In show six of The X Factor during the VT, Perrie fell off the box she was standing on. Kelly Rowland saw it and mouthed to check that she was all right.

GUILTY PLEASURE: Fancies the cartoon John Smith in Disney's *Pocahontas!*

TRIVIA MIX: Between Boot Camp and the Judges' Houses, all four girls moved into Perrie's home to rehearse.

THE PERFECT MIX
LEIGH-ANNE

LEIGH-ANNE PINNOCK

HOMETOWN: High Wycombe.

STAR SIGN: Libra.

SHOPAHOLIC: Leigh-Anne's favourite shops are River Island and New Era. Back in her hometown, River Island closed to let her browse the rails in peace and privacy. Now that's customer service!

SECRET TALENT: Songwriting.

BEFORE THE X FACTOR: Leigh-Anne worked as a waitress in Pizza Hut.

FIRST AUDITION: *Only Girl (In The World)* by Rihanna.

MOST EMBARRASSING MOMENT: At a secret gig in London, she walked into a TV and bashed her head in front of the audience.

GUILTY PLEASURE: Justin Bieber – she had posters of him stuck on the walls of her room.

TRIVIA MIX: When Rihanna guested on The X Factor, she walked past Leigh-Anne, did a double-take and said her hair was 'awesome'!

THE PERFECT MIX
JESY

JESY NELSON

HOMETOWN: Romford.

STAR SIGN: Gemini.

SHOPAHOLIC: Jesy loves to buy clothes at Topshop and London's Camden Market.

SECRET TALENT: Beatboxing.

BEFORE THE X FACTOR: She worked as a barmaid.

FIRST AUDITION: *Bust Your Windows* by Jazmine Sullivan.

MOST EMBARRASSING MOMENT: When her nan appeared on The Xtra Factor and revealed to the nation that Jesy once drank a cup of wee! Eww!

GUILTY PLEASURE: *TOWIE.*

TRIVIA MIX: Jesy has a bit of an obsession with trainers and owns over 90 pairs.

THE PERFECT MIX
JADE

JADE THIRLWALL

HOMETOWN: South Shields.

STAR SIGN: Capricorn.

SHOPAHOLIC: Jade is a self-confessed vintage and Zara addict.

SECRET TALENT: Painting and drawing – she scored an A* in her Art GCSE.

BEFORE THE X FACTOR: Jade was a student and took part in various singing contests and gigs in her area.

FIRST AUDITION: *I Want to Hold Your Hand* by The Beatles.

MOST EMBARRASSING MOMENT: During the dress rehearsal for *Don't Stop The Music*, her hotpants split and EVERYONE noticed! She had to get extra fabric sewn into them as they were too tight.

GUILTY PLEASURE: Watching Disney DVDs and eating lasagne.

TRIVIA MIX: Jade tried out for The X Factor three times before she got lucky. Search Katie 4 Harry (Styles) – Xtra Factor on YouTube and Jade pops up in the video.

DREAMS CAN COME TRUE

THE GIRLS' JOURNEY started when they auditioned alongside thousands of hopefuls for The X Factor 2011, hoping to become successful solo artists. The girls turned up at their separate auditions a mixture of nerves and excitement. After all, this could be their chance to secure a record deal and change their lives beyond all recognition. The judges liked all four of the girls and they were put through to bootcamp. They were over the moon; it seemed too good to be true. And all too soon it seemed like it was. Although all four of the girls undeniably had star presence, it was felt they lacked the confidence needed to be soloists. The girls were told they were being put into groups – Leigh-Anne and Jade were put into a group called Orion and Perrie and Jesy were placed in a band called Faux Pas. Although they tried to hide it, the girls were gutted. Not surprising when you think that girl bands had never done well on The X Factor in the past.

"It was definitely in the back of our minds,"
says Jade. "I don't think any of us wanted to be
in a girl group at first."

Despite this, they were all determined not to let this knock-back stop them. They were prepared to do whatever it took to get through to the next stage. Leigh-Anne, Jade, Jesy and Perrie put everything they had into their band

performances, but it just wasn't enough. A devastated Orion and Faux Pas were told that, for them, the competition had ended.

"To get that far and get rejected…" shudders
Leigh-Anne. "Worst feeling in the world."

But the story wasn't quite over. Backstage, the judges were having second thoughts about their decision. They knew the competition needed a young, fresh girl group and there were four girls that they just couldn't stop thinking about. Jade, Perrie, Leigh-Anne and Jesy were called back to the stage.

"They just knew they belonged together."

**"We had no idea what was going on,"
laughs Perrie. "My legs were like, argghhh!"**

As the girls walked out on to the stage grasping each others hands nervously, there was a sudden sense of electricity in the air. The judges couldn't believe how much they looked like a band. After a moment's pause, Kelly Rowland spoke; she had no idea then just how prophetic her words would be.

"You're probably wondering what you're doing up there, huh? We truly feel that the four of you could bring something very special to this competition. Do you think you can work together?"

As the girls stared at each other in disbelief, all of their worries about being in a girl band unexpectedly melted away. Somehow they just knew they belonged together. That, like Kelly had said, this really could be the start of something incredibly special.

Jesy says, "I just remember us looking at each other and thinking 'this is going to work'."

Immediately the girls got on brilliantly, laughing and mucking around with each other. But it was more than that; they were all professionals at heart and were obviously hungry for success. And when the girls found out that Tulisa was to be their X Factor mentor, the last piece of the jigsaw fell into place.

"Like us, she had a lot to prove," says Jesy. "She maybe wasn't as well known as the other judges. More than that, she didn't want to change us, she wanted us to be just the same."

"That was the challenge. Being ourselves and letting the public know who we were," adds Jade.

The band was in place, the girls decided on a name – Rhythmix – but there was still another challenge to get through – the Judges' Houses. The girls all moved in together and spent every single day running through their songs. Each little mistake had to be criticised and corrected. The girls knew what a big chance they'd been given and they weren't about to blow it.

It worked. From their first live performance at the Judges' Houses in front of Tulisa and

Jessie J, right through to the first live show, it was obvious that these girls were something special. Together, they had so much talent, ambition and enthusiasm that failure was never really on the cards. The journey wasn't always easy though. They were forced to change their name halfway through the competition due to a charity already being called Rhythmix. But the girls won the hearts and the votes of the whole nation. They proved that the music scene needs young, positive girl groups. When the girls were growing up, they'd had the Spice Girls to look up to. Pop fans needed a group like that. A girl band who could deliver songs with bags of energy and dance moves and who were also down-to-earth and genuine.

Little Mix made X Factor history as weeks went on, becoming the first all-female band to ever make it into the top six and also the only X Factor contestants never to be in the bottom two. And in December 2011, millions of people watched as Little Mix became the first girl band ever to win the competition. It had never happened like this before and never to a girl group – Little Mix had well and truly smashed The X Factor's curse on girl bands. Their winner's single, *Cannonball,* hit the No. 1 position in three different countries. It was obvious that Little Mix were an absolute, unstoppable, undeniable, certified hit.

The time was definitely right for Little Mix, but no-one could have predicted the way that Little Mix fever would erupt and how the whole world would jump to its feet and welcome them like all-conquering heroines. And their journey was just beginning.

LITTLE MIX QUIZ

1
What was Tulisa's nickname for Little Mix?

A. Little Muffins

B. Baby Crumpets

C. Tiny Toasts

2
Which song did they sing in the first live show?

A. *Super Bass*

B. *Don't Let Go*

C. *Cannonball*

3
Who is the oldest member of the group?

A. Leigh-Anne

B. Perrie

C. Jesy

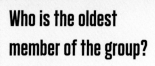

4
Who were they against in The X Factor finals?

A. One Direction

B. Marcus Collins

C. Kitty Brucknell

5
Which two members are from South Shields?

A. Jade and Jesy

B. Perrie and Leigh-Anne

C. Jade and Perrie

6
Who is Perrie named after?

A. Perrier water

B. Her grandad

C. Steve Perry

ANSWERS

1.a 3.c 5.c 7.a 9.b
2.a 4.b 6.c 8.a 10.c

22

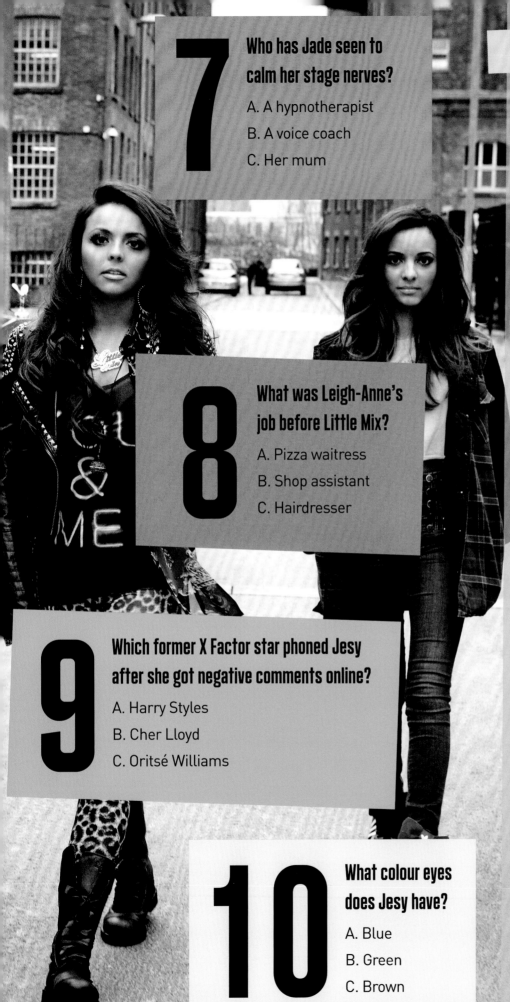

7 Who has Jade seen to calm her stage nerves?

A. A hypnotherapist

B. A voice coach

C. Her mum

8 What was Leigh-Anne's job before Little Mix?

A. Pizza waitress

B. Shop assistant

C. Hairdresser

9 Which former X Factor star phoned Jesy after she got negative comments online?

A. Harry Styles

B. Cher Lloyd

C. Oritsé Williams

10 What colour eyes does Jesy have?

A. Blue

B. Green

C. Brown

HOW DID YOU DO?

0 - 3

You love Little Mix, but you don't know that much about the girls. Put *Cannonball* on your MP3 player immediately, whack up the volume to full, turn to the beginning of this book and start reading it. Oh and repeat, "Little Mix rock!" ten times every night before you go to bed.

4 - 7

Hmm, not a bad score, but you could do better. You like the songs and you know the girls' last names, but it's the little details that make up the whole picture, you know. You can't call yourself a true fan unless you know everything from what Leigh-Anne likes for breakfast to what time Perrie goes to bed.

8 - 10

You are a true Little Mix fan. You know all their songs by heart, where they live and even the names of their childhood friends. Give yourself a pat on the back and rest assured in the knowledge that Little Mix would be proud to introduce you to their mothers. Well done you!

LIFE AFTER THE X FACTOR

FAME MIGHT HAVE come quickly to Little Mix, but they've certainly taken to it like naturals. Perhaps the most surprising thing about their success is that there's been absolutely no change in any of the girls. They're still the same home-loving, small-town, big-hearted girls they've always been. They're completely professional and they know that only hard work will keep them at the top. At heart, they're still the fans, the ordinary girls, who have made it big. Like any other girls, they worry about pimples, bite their nails and fret about running up huge mobile phone bills while they're away from home. Their heroes are their families, especially their mums – the Mummy Mixers – and they still have their oldest friends

with them all the way. Life as a celebrity can become overwhelming and it's sometimes hard to hang on to yourself. But Little Mix are keeping it real no matter what the crazy world of pop throws at them.

As Jade says, "There's no way we'd become divas. It's just not our style."

As soon as The X Factor finished, there was no time to lose. There was a long hard slog ahead before Little Mix's post-X Factor career could really be launched. The girls' diaries were packed with an endless list of interviews, appearances and gigs. There was choreography to learn, songs to be practised, anything and everything that would give them an edge over their competition.

"We thought being in The X Factor was crazy!" laughs Perrie. "What did we know?"

With everything else in place, it was time to get down to some serious songwriting and recording. Little Mix had to establish a sound that really set them apart. And that meant finding some professionals to help them turn what they did naturally into studio magic. Richard 'Biff' Stannard is one of the best in the business, with the knack of coaxing the best performances possible from singers. And the girls even managed to secure the services of a songwriter who penned one hit that means a lot to them – Andrea Martin, who wrote En Vogue's song, *Don't Let Go*. The real fun began as they got into the studio and really began to find their identity.

"We're going a bit urban, old school with a bit of pop," Perrie said at the time. "We wanna bring back old school harmonies. And Jesy beat-boxes and Leigh-Anne raps, so we're trying out different things."

They spent most of the spring recording songs, crafting a sound that was totally fresh and unique. They came up with a record crammed full of potential hits and the girls are justifiably proud of their first album.

...Next stop: the top of the world!

GIRLS TOGETHER

The girls may have embraced life as famous pop stars, but they're still just like you and me!

Do you still get to do normal stuff?

Jade: "I still get to see my mum and friends and go out. We're all really normal. The only thing that's not normal is that we perform to thousands of people."

Perrie: "It can be a bit more hectic if we're out with Jesy because she gets recognised a lot. One of my favourite things to do is to go to the arcade with my friend Katherine and spend loads of time playing the 2p machines or bowling. That's never going to change."

Leigh-Anne: "When I'm back home I'll still go shopping with my friends, and go into Watford and go raving. We are still normal girls and that's not going to change. We're never going to get ahead of ourselves. My family and friends will make sure of that, and we've got each other to keep us grounded."

Jesy: "Things like shopping are different because we get recognised and people ask for our autographs. But we still go out and eat and sleep and all of those things and we want to stay true to who we are."

What's your favourite TV show?

Perrie: "I grew up watching *Friends* and I still love it now. More recently I've got into *The OC* and I can't stop watching it. I need to get the next series as soon as I can! *Saved By The Bell* is my all-time favourite TV show!"

Jesy: "*Friends* is my favourite too. It makes me laugh and when I watch it I feel like they're my friends. I've watched every episode a million times and I never get bored of it."

Jade: "I love *The Fresh Prince of Bel Air* and *Family Guy*. They both really make me laugh. I also love *Keeping Up With The Kardashians*."

Perrie: "I love my nana's roast on a Sunday and I love homemade curries. Chicken tikka masala is my absolute favourite."

Jade: "I love my mum's Sunday roasts. Actually I like anything she makes me."

Leigh-Anne: "Nachos, with all the trimmings. Sour cream, salsa, cheese – the lot."

What's your guilty pleasure?

Jade: "Sudoku. And puzzle books generally."

Leigh-Anne: "Justin Bieber. I'm actually a bit in love with him. I know I shouldn't like him, but I do. He's a wicked performer."

Jesy: "Easter eggs. I said in an interview once I love them so I keep getting given them and it's great."

Perrie: "I love teddies. I've got loads on my bed at home because it makes me feel safer. I also take them around with me and at the moment I've got a really cute penguin that my friend gave me. I love penguins."

Leigh-Anne: "I love *Waterloo Road*. I don't have time to see it any more, but I used to watch it with my mum religiously."

What's your favourite movie?

Leigh-Anne: "*Titanic*. It's an iconic film and I cry every time I watch it."

Jade: "I love all Disney films and also a really old movie called *Who Will Love My Children*? that was my granddad's favourite."

Perrie: "*The Notebook*. It's so romantic. I like to watch it with a big bowl of ice cream."

Jesy: "I've got loads, but I would say *Taken*. Liam Neeson's in it and it's such a good film."

What's your favourite meal?

Jesy: "Nando's. I always have a quarter chicken with lemon and herbs, chips and rice."

"We've got each other to keep us grounded."

A IS FOR ATTITUDE.
These girls have some serious swagger.

B IS FOR BURPING.
Perrie is the band's biggest burper.

C IS FOR COOKIES.
Because everyone knows Jade loves her biscuits.

D IS FOR *DON'T LET GO.*
Their version is AMAZE BALLS – it gives us shivers every time!

E IS FOR ENTERTAINING.
Their banter is legendary!

F IS FOR FRIENDSHIP.
The closeness between the girls radiates wherever they go.

G IS FOR GIRL POWER.
They are living proof of what can happen when girls have each other's backs.

H IS FOR THEIR SPINETINGLINGLY SOLID HARMONIES.
Have you heard these girls sing a capella?!

I IS FOR 'INTERESTING'.
One of the girls' favourite words.

J IS FOR JESSIE J.
She would love to write for Little Mix. "They're great girls and have brilliant voices," she says.

K IS FOR KEEP ON GOING NO MATTER WHAT.
These girls never let setbacks keep them down.

L IS FOR LITTLE MUFFINS.
Tulisa's nickname for the band.

M IS FOR MORNINGS.
The girls really hate them.

N IS FOR NANDO'S.
If Jesy could only eat one thing for the rest of her life this would be it.

O IS FOR OLIVES.
Perrie hates them, but for some reason still eats them. Crazy chick.

P IS FOR PRACTICE MAKES PERFECT.
It really does.

Q IS FOR QUEUEING.

The girls will never forget waiting for hours in the X Factor queue.

R IS FOR RHYTHMIX.

The girls' original band name.

S IS FOR SPICE GIRLS.

All four girls love them and the Spice Girls love Little Mix right back!

T IS FOR TULISA.

"She's more than a mentor, she's a friend for life," says Jade.

U IS FOR THE GIRLS' UNIQUE VOICES.

We can't get enough of them.

V IS FOR VIDEO DIARIES.

The girls' video diaries for The Xtra Factor were laugh-out-loud fabulous.

W IS FOR WRITING SONGS.

The girls love writing them... and we can't wait to hear them.

X IS FOR X FACTOR WINNERS.

The first girl band EVER to win the show. Little Mix, we salute you!

Y IS FOR YOU LOT!

The girls love, love, LOVE their Little Mixers!

Z IS FOR ZZZ...

The girls are going to be so busy over the next few years, they'd be wise to get some sleep while they can!

LITTLE M·I·X STYLE

THE LITTLE MIXES are quickly developing their own sense of statement style. The trainer-loving popettes have always dressed to impress as individuals, but as a group they've transformed into fully-fledged fashionistas. Yet they are the kind of girls every other girl can identify with, they just seem so normal, just like the girls next door.

They may all have come together as individual artists, but amazingly they fit together. They are all definitely one-of-a-kinds and they all dress differently and yet somehow they look like they belong together. They don't need to be carbon copies of each other.

As Perrie says, "If everyone stayed the same and dressed the same, it would be so boring."

Having been brought together as a band, each member brought their own unique style to The X Factor table - something the girls have been keen to cling on to, despite being styled together as a group. The girls still look completely different from each other, but they still look like a band. It just works.

One thing's for certain, whether they're in sweat pants or designer dresses, they always look a million dollars.

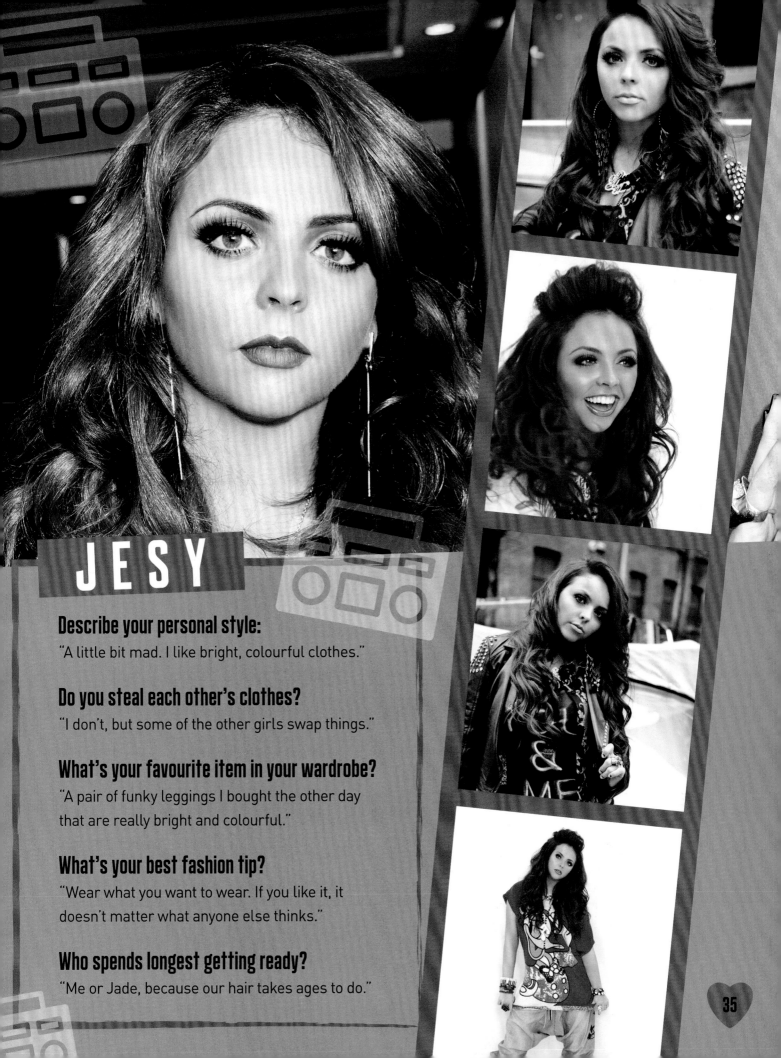

JESY

Describe your personal style:

"A little bit mad. I like bright, colourful clothes."

Do you steal each other's clothes?

"I don't, but some of the other girls swap things."

What's your favourite item in your wardrobe?

"A pair of funky leggings I bought the other day that are really bright and colourful."

What's your best fashion tip?

"Wear what you want to wear. If you like it, it doesn't matter what anyone else thinks."

Who spends longest getting ready?

"Me or Jade, because our hair takes ages to do."

JADE

Describe your personal style:
"Geeky, cute, cool and urban."

Do you steal each other's clothes?
"Occasionally! Me and Leigh swapped clothes at X Factor Boot Camp. Us girls will often go out shopping separately and come back with the same thing. It's really weird."

What's your favourite item in your wardrobe?
"Bows and braces."

What's your best fashion tip?
"Definitely follow your own style. You don't feel good if you're wearing something you don't feel comfortable in."

Who spends longest getting ready?
"Definitely Jesy!"

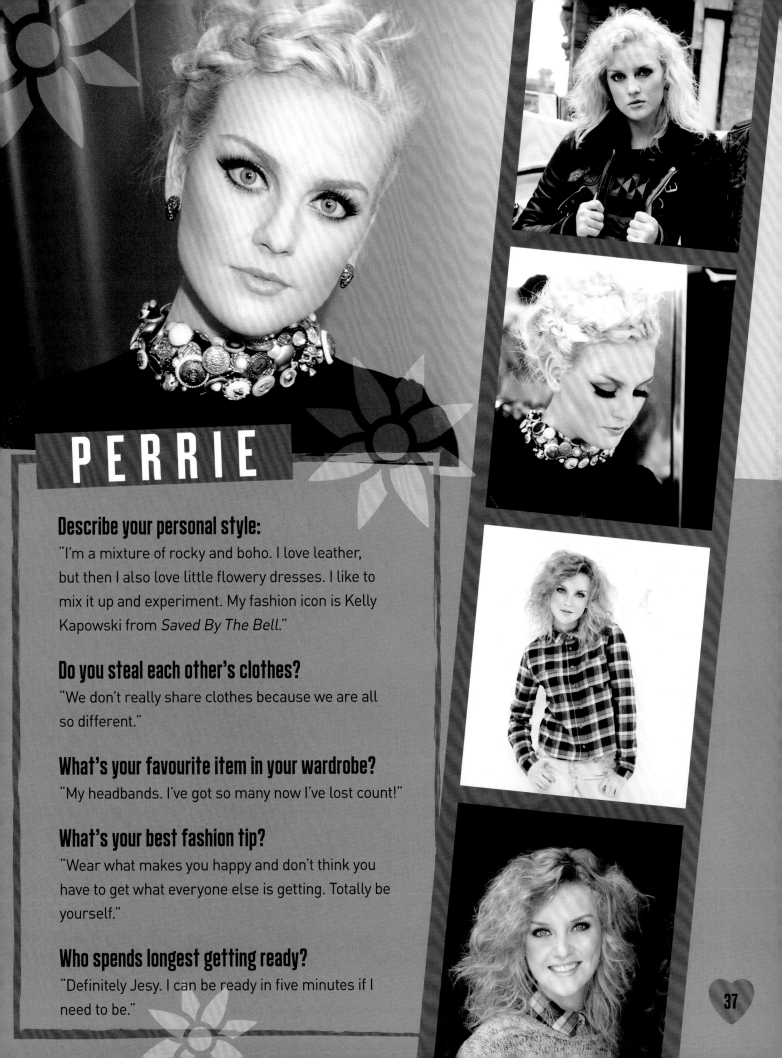

PERRIE

Describe your personal style:
"I'm a mixture of rocky and boho. I love leather, but then I also love little flowery dresses. I like to mix it up and experiment. My fashion icon is Kelly Kapowski from *Saved By The Bell*."

Do you steal each other's clothes?
"We don't really share clothes because we are all so different."

What's your favourite item in your wardrobe?
"My headbands. I've got so many now I've lost count!"

What's your best fashion tip?
"Wear what makes you happy and don't think you have to get what everyone else is getting. Totally be yourself."

Who spends longest getting ready?
"Definitely Jesy. I can be ready in five minutes if I need to be."

LEIGH-ANNE

Describe your personal style:
"I'm a mix of Rihanna and the Fresh Prince."

Do you steal each other's clothes?
"I don't need to because I've got so many clothes I don't know what to do with them all!"

What's your favourite item in your wardrobe?
"I love all of my trainers and hats."

What's your best fashion tip?
"Old school clothes and bright patterns always look cool."

Who spends longest getting ready?
"Jesy because she always spends so long doing her hair. It takes forever."

WHICH LITTLE MIXER WOULD YOU BE?

1 What's your favourite choice of outfit?

A. A pretty dress.
B. Some funky leggings.
C. Something accessorised with a funky bow.
D. Anything old school with Tims.

2 What's your favourite meal?

A. A huge curry.
B. Nando's.
C. Roast dinner with all the trimmings.
D. Nachos with sour cream, salsa cheese and Mexican chicken.

3 What's your favourite type of movie?

A. A rom-com.
B. A thriller or romance.
C. Anything by Disney.
D. A real weepy or scary movie.

4 How would your friends describe you?

A. Always happy and smiling.
B. Funny and always there for them.
C. Cute and feisty.
D. Honest and kind-hearted.

5 What do you like doing in your spare time?

A. Shopping in Topshop.
B. Shopping in Camden Market.
C. Watching a Disney DVD.
D. Singing along to Justin Bieber.

Mostly A)s: Perrie

Always up for fun, you have a happy, outgoing attitude to life. Your smile is completely infectious and can light up any room, à la Perrie.

Mostly B)s: Jesy

Your friends quite rightly describe you as the nicest person ever. Like Jesy you make everyone feel at ease and all your pals know they can come to you with any problems.

Mostly C)s: Jade

Your mates know you are sweet, innocent, cute and more than a little bit cheeky. Just like Jade you have a feisty side and aren't afraid to show it.

Mostly D)s: Leigh-Anne

Just like Leigh-Anne you are amazingly kind-hearted and generous. You're incredibly loyal too, and are always there for your circle of friends.

SAY WHAT?

The weird and wonderful things that come out of the mouths of our favourite girls.

"I don't understand what just happened. I think we just won..."

PERRIE

"I don't eat crusts because my hair is curly enough as it is."

JADE

"Our music will be a little mix of everything."

LEIGH-ANNE

"I was just thinking please don't put me in a girl group, I won't fit in at all."

JADE

JESY

"I want us all to be together. I don't want a four-bedroom place. I love living in the same room!"

"How do they get the salad in the box if it's already sealed?"

PERRIE

"The good thing about being called Little Muffins is you get a lot of muffins."

JADE

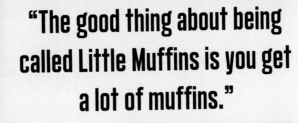

LITTLE MIX REVEALED

WE CAUGHT UP WITH THE GIRLS FOR AN EXCLUSIVE CHAT!

Is it hard to be role models?

Jade: "We didn't plan to be role models, but it just happened. We were just being ourselves and girls said how much we inspired them so that's fine by us. It's lovely to know people think of us like that, but it does come with a bit of pressure because people will be watching everything we do."

Jesy: "At the same time, we're not perfect and I think a lot of people can relate to that as well."

Leigh-Anne: "We're just about having fun."

What's the hardest thing about being in the public eye?

Perrie: "Probably not seeing our families and friends."

Leigh-Anne: "Also, being in the public eye all the time, someone's going to have an opinion or comment about something you're doing. We're just going to have to get used to it because there will be negative comments."

Jade: "At the beginning it was really hard, but now we see some of the other stuff that gets printed and we just laugh. For every time that someone writes something nasty, we get so many fans that are nice to us all of the time."

Jesy: "And we must be doing something right if they want to write about us."

Who's your favourite band or artist?

Jade: "The Spice Girls because they were my dream role models when I was younger. My entire bedroom was decorated with Spice Girls stuff. I also love Beyoncé because I think she's the most amazing artist in the world at the moment."

Leigh-Anne: "That's so hard! I'm going to have to say Rihanna. Her music is amazing and I know how hard she works and I really respect her. She's also beautiful and a great style icon. I adored her when she first came out and I'd

love her to bring back more of her Bajan roots, because I'm Bajan and Jamaican."

Perrie: "It varies with me. I love Journey because I was brought up listening to them and Steve Perry's voice is out of this world. I loved JoJo when I was growing up and I like all the big divas like Beyoncé and Mariah Carey nowadays."

Jesy: "Beyoncé because she's so different and when she performs she doesn't care what anyone else thinks. I love her music and I'm really inspired by her."

What would you say to anyone who wants to be on The X Factor?

Jade: "Do it. And if you don't get through the first time do it again and again and again until you do."

Jesy: "Be prepared, don't hold back – and enjoy every single minute."

Perrie: "Be ready and be prepared and look at it as a great experience. Don't get too caught up in the stress. Take a step back and enjoy it."

Leigh-Anne: "Go for it. Be individual, be who you are, give everything you can give."

How do you think you're coping with being famous?

Jesy: "I think we're coping really well. We're having loads of fun and really enjoying it."

Leigh-Anne: "I always wanted to be famous. I wanted to be a singer, but I wanted everything that goes with it too. I love being in magazines and meeting fans and everything. It's so strange that people want to know about my life now! I know things will get crazier but I think I'll be fine."

"I still don't feel famous."

Perrie: "I still don't feel famous. I feel really normal and I don't get recognised very much when I walk down the street. If I ever tried to be a diva my mum would have a word with me. We're all from really normal families so they keep us grounded."

Jade: "I think we're all coping really well. We take each day as it comes. We know how lucky we are so we don't complain."

You meet some great people – do you have any celeb crushes?

Perrie: "Johnny Depp, but I haven't met him yet. He's the man of my dreams."

Jade: "I like Labrinth. I'm really embarrassed because I always talk about him. I just think he's really cool. His style is great and his music is amazing. I also like Will Smith and Denzel Washington is lovely. I know he's old, but he's gorgeous."

Leigh-Anne: "Justin Bieber, without a doubt. When I saw him for the first time singing *Baby* on The X Factor that was it. I love that clean-cut look. I love pretty boys and I love his music. "

Jesy: "I fancy Plan B. I met him and he was amazing. He was so charming. I like guys who are a bit Cockney. I like Danny Dyer too."

What were the best/worst bits of the tour?

Perrie: "The best thing was performing and seeing all of the people who came along. I loved the meets and greets because we got to see the fans. The worst bit was probably having to get up and travel a lot. I tried to sleep on the coach, but it was quite hard."

Leigh-Anne: "The best bit was performing every night, doing something you love and seeing the fans singing along to your songs. I don't think there were any bad parts. I loved it."

Jade: "It was so nice being reunited with everyone again, but the worst thing was probably being tired quite a lot because it was pretty non-stop."

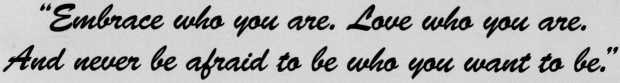

"Embrace who you are. Love who you are. And never be afraid to be who you want to be."

Can you describe your 'sound'?

Jesy: "Fun, fresh and different."

Leigh-Anne: "Pop, R&B and hip-hop merged. We're bringing back the old school harmonies in the style of En Vogue, TLC and SWV."

Jade: "We're feel-good, uplifting and inspiring."

Perrie: "We're quirky and edgy with soul harmonies."

Any songs you'd particularly like to cover?

Jesy: "Emile Sandé's *Daddy*. It's so lovely and she's wicked."

Leigh-Anne: "I agree with Jesy. I'd like to cover Emile Sandé's *Daddy*. It's such a brilliant song."

Perrie: "I'd like to take a really old song and sample it on one of our tracks. Something like *Eye of the Tiger* would be amazing."

Jade: "I'd love to bring an old Motown song up to date. A Diana Ross song would be brilliant. Or maybe we could do our own version of a Spice Girls song."

Who would you most like to duet with?

Jade: "Rizzle Kicks or Ed Sheeran would be cool."

Leigh-Anne: "Rihanna, of course!"

Perrie: "Steve Perry from Journey."

Jesy: "Chris Brown because he's an all-round amazing performer."

If you could give young girls one piece of advice what would it be?

Jade: "You will blossom! I used to hate myself at school. I thought I was disgusting and spotty and horrible, but you change as you get older. It's not the end of the world if you've got a few spots. Also listen to your mum because she knows best."

Leigh-Anne: "Believe in yourself. I've got 'Believe' tattooed on my neck because I think if you don't believe in yourself no-one else will."

Jesy: "Embrace who you are. Love who you are. And never be afraid to be who you want to be. If you've got a dream, go for it and don't let anyone tell you that you can't do something."

Perrie: "Don't let anything take away your self-esteem, and don't ever think you have to change because you're perfect as you are."

QUICK-FIRE INTERVIEW

DO YOU HAVE A NICKNAME?

Jesy: "The girls call me Whining Willow because I like to have a good moan sometimes. We've all got nicknames for each other – Leigh-Anne is Diva Dibbs, Jade's called Poopy and Perrie is called Stressy Sue."

Leigh-Anne: "I also get called Leigh-Leigh. My dad and my aunties always used to call me that when I was young and it's stuck."

Perrie: "I get called either Pez, Pezza or Pezhead after the sweets. I also get called Perrie the platypus on Twitter after the one on *Phineas and Ferb*."

Jade: "When I was younger I used to get called Pickle, but now I get called Poopy."

WHAT'S THE STRANGEST THING YOU'VE EVER BEEN GIVEN?

Leigh-Anne: "I've only been given nice things so far."

Jade: "Same here. We get lovely gifts."

Jesy: "I haven't been given anything strange, but I know that one guy got a heart with the letter P tattooed on his hand because he's a really big fan of Perrie's."

Perrie: "That's definitely the most unusual thing someone's done for me. I never expected that to happen."

TELL US ONE INTERESTING THING WE DON'T KNOW ABOUT YOU.

Leigh-Anne: "I was a senior prefect and head girl in Sixth Form."

Perrie: "I've got no sense of smell. But I think most people probably know that about me now."

Jade: "I want to get a tattoo of a bow behind my ear, as well as a few others. I'm also good at tap dancing."

Jesy: "I was in the film *About A Boy* when I was younger. I was only an extra, but I was in the assembly hall when he was singing, and in the playground when he was being picked on. I met Hugh Grant and he was lovely. At one point the camera zooms right in on my face, although you would never recognise me. I think I was only about ten at the time."

WHAT'S IN YOUR HANDBAG?

Leigh-Anne: "My life! Hair stuff, deodorant, my iPod because I'm always listening to music, my phone and my purse."

Perrie: "My phone, a hairband, make-up, music... Whatever I can fit in."

Jesy: "Hairspray, hairbrushes, make-up, my purse, phone, sunglasses and anything else I can fit in there."

Jade: "My whole life is in mine. My phone, my purse, a mini pharmacy, tickets for things from years ago and my chargers. My bag is like a Mary Poppins bag. It's falling apart, but I can't get rid of it because I love it. If I could fit my family in there and carry them around with me, I would."

IF YOU COULD ONLY TAKE ONE THING WITH YOU TO A DESERT ISLAND WHAT WOULD IT BE?

Jade: "A Sudoku book to pass the time."

Jesy: "My mobile phone, so I could call and get rescued."

Perrie: "I'd take an M&S so I'd have loads of food and clothes to choose from. I could also live in it!"

Leigh-Anne: "Toothpaste. I'm really hygienic and at least I could have a bath in the sea and then use my finger to brush my teeth."

NO DOUBT ABOUT IT, THESE GIRLS ARE THE BEST OF FRIENDS...

What do you like most about each other?

Jesy: "I love that they're all so funny. I'm in stitches every single day when I'm around them."

Leigh-Anne: "Jesy and I are so close and we always share a room if we can. She's been through a lot and I can really relate to her. I can talk to her about anything. Perrie, I just love. She's so happy all the time and she gives me really good advice. She's got a really good head on her shoulders and her laughter is infectious. Jade is such a little cutie. She's got a real innocence about her, but she can be feisty and she'll say it like it is. She can stand up for herself."

Perrie: "When Jesy's in a good mood, everyone is in a good mood. She could make the whole world smile. Jade is my little Geordie lass and she's my little home rock. Leigh-Anne is amazing. She's so funny and she doesn't even know it. She says I'm a ray of sunshine, but I think she's the same. We're all just there for each other. They're my sisters from other misters and if I have a problem I can talk to any of them."

Jade: "Leigh-Anne is so honest and mature and smart and kind-hearted. Jesy makes me laugh whether she's in a good or bad mood and she will defend any of us to the earth. Perrie is such a happy person. Whenever she's upset it really worries everyone because she's always cheerful. If ever I feel a bit down I go and see her and she makes me feel better. She also has no idea how talented she is. Her voice is incredible. They're all really beautiful girls as well."

"She could make the whole world smile."

What do you find funny/annoying about each other?

Leigh-Anne: "Jesy has the ability to talk in every single accent under the sun, but when I attempt it, it doesn't work. Jesy and I also have this Hillbilly thing we do which makes me laugh. We all have Hillbilly names. I'm Betsy, Jesy is Wilma, Perrie is Bam Bam and Jade is Edna. The only annoying thing about any of them is that Jesy wakes up really early and blow-dries her hair. Jade and Perrie are the laziest and Perrie wakes up five minutes before we need to leave to go anywhere."

Perrie: "I love that Leigh-Anne is a bit of a klutz. I find them all funny though. They really don't annoy me at all. I don't like being woken up, but we all have to get up at some point to work."

Jesy: "I don't like it when Perrie burps or when Leigh-Anne burps and blows it in people's faces. Jade doesn't really do anything annoying."

Jade: "If Jesy's in a bad mood it can be a bit scary. Leigh-Anne sometimes word vomits a bit and Perrie doesn't realise how good she is at singing. She's so incredible on stage."

What other member of the band would you like to be?

Leigh-Anne: "Jesy, because she's one of the best performers I've ever seen. Every time I see her perform she gives 100% and she inspires me."

Jesy: "Leigh-Anne because she's one of the loveliest people I've ever met. She'll put anyone before herself, and will always put her friends before any boy. She's also an amazing, strong performer. And she's beautiful too."

Jade: "I'd be Perrie because of her voice, or Jesy because of her gorgeous figure."

Perrie: "I'd be happy to be any of them. I think they're all amazing in different ways. The best thing is that we've always got each other."

LIVE YOUR LIFE
THE LITTLE MIX WAY

The girls have learnt a lot on their journey to superstardom. They want to share it with you:

FIND YOUR OWN STYLE

The girls have never been slaves to trends, preferring to wear what suits them instead. As Leigh-Anne says: "If you've got your own individual style then go for it and don't let anyone tell you it's wrong. Embrace it. We have all got our own look. The key is being yourself." Go girls!

YOUR MUM IS ALWAYS RIGHT

The girls are really close to their mums, who have supported them throughout their X Factor journeys and beyond. As Perrie says, "I always wanted to be a singer, but I never had the confidence to do it. It was my mum who made me believe in myself."

BIG UP THE SISTERHOOD

Little Mix are all about girl power. They are best friends and are there for each other through good or bad. They haven't got time for the haters and think girls should always have each other's backs. "Because it's about time, isn't it, that girls liked girls," says Jade. We couldn't agree more.

"If you've got your own individual style then go for it and don't let anyone tell you it's wrong. Embrace it."

KEEP IT REAL

Despite being the hottest girl band on the planet right now , they are still completely and utterly normal . "There's no way we'd ever become divas. It's just not our style," says Jesy. That's one of the reasons we love them so much, they're the kind of girls you could totally imagine living next door to. #wishing.

GOOD THINGS COME TO THOSE WHO WAIT

Jade was rejected from The X Factor three times before she got lucky. But after every knockback she picked herself up, brushed herself down and tried again. "If you absolutely love something, don't take no for an answer and just keep going," she says. "Things have a way of working out for the best."

EMBRACE WHO YOU ARE

They may be fully-fledged popstars, but the girls still have insecurities just like every other female. They don't let negative thoughts get them down, though. "Everybody wants what they don't have," says Jesy. "At the end of the day, what you have inside is much more beautiful than what's on the outside." Here, here.

LITTLE MIX
AND YOU

THE GIRLS REALLY love their fans and are so grateful to each and every one of you!

You have such amazing fans. What's the nicest thing a fan has ever done for you?

Leigh-Anne: "We've got an incredible fan called Yaz who made me a snap-back hat with Leigh written on it. It probably cost a lot of money and I thought it was so sweet."

Jesy: "Some fans made us a huge book charting everything from our first auditions right up to now. It's got pictures and magazine articles and it's massive. They know everything about us."

Perrie: "I love it when our fans make fan books with quotes and pictures of what we've been up to. It's so nice to be reminded of what we've done. Things are so hectic that we sometimes forget the journey we've been on. It's really cute that they sit there and make these lovely things for us."

Jade: "I love the scrapbooks, they always make me smile. I also love it when we get letters from fans saying that we've helped them in some way. We get loads from girls who say they've been bullied or they weren't confident, and because of us they're feeling better. That's the most rewarding part of what we do."

Why do you think your fans connect with you so much?

Perrie: "We've never tried to be something we're not. What's so amazing is that we were in The X Factor because we love to sing and we want girls to see that you can look up to someone who is real. We haven't been in the industry that long and we're still down to earth. We've been thrown in the deep end a bit so we're still learning too."

Jesy: "We're not trying to be anything we're not. I think that's a really big reason why we won The X Factor. We're relatable and we have problems just like everyone else. We're also fun and we like a laugh."

Jade: "Girls are never intimidated when we meet them. They'll always come over to us and give us a hug like they know us. It's so nice that they feel comfortable."

Leigh-Anne: "We're funny and we have our own individual personalities. I think when people watch our YouTube videos they can see that we're just like them and we like to have a laugh and take the mick."

What would you like to say to your fans?

Jade: "You rock!"

Jesy: "Just a huge, huge thanks for all the support you've given us from the start. We wouldn't be here if it wasn't for you. We love you all so much."

Jade: "We want to thank everyone that has supported Little Mix, it means the world to us."

Perrie: "We have the best fans EVER. They've never judged us and they feel they can relate to us, which is the main thing. They're the fans we'll have for life."

THE FUTURE'S SO BRIGHT, LITTLE MIX ARE WEARING SHADES...

LOOKING AT HOW much they've already achieved, it's easy to forget how far they've come in such a short period of time. And the way things are going Little Mix's shooting star shows no sign of falling. Their profile keeps growing and growing as they continue a feverish pace of touring, performing and promotion. Little Mix are one of the busiest, hardest working bands in pop, and they know if they carry on making good music, the sky's the limit.

And you can tell they're loving every minute. Their music shows how much they've grown. They're that little bit wiser, far more confident and completely in control. You only have to watch them perform to see that they're having the time of their lives. They feel every single line they sing and are giving it their all, that's why they connect so much with everyone who hears them.

They're young, fun and exactly what pop music should be about. But it's not just about music, Little Mix have shown us just what can happen with a little bit of self-belief and the power of friendship. They've shown us that you can go against expectations and create your own opportunities for success.

There's absolutely no doubt that Little Mix are going to be here for a long time to come.

LAST WORD
FROM THE GIRLS

WHAT ARE YOUR HOPES FOR THE FUTURE?

PERRIE

"For us to be the biggest girl band in the world and become icons."

LEIGH-ANNE

"We want to have fun, inspire people and make incredible music that people can identify with."

JESY

"I want the band to do amazingly well and for us all to be happy."

JADE

"I want us to have a long career. We want to be able to crack Europe and America and Asia. We want to go global and be able to support our families for the rest of our lives."

And they've only just begun...